MAXnotes®

Herman Melville's

Billy Budd

Text by
Miriam Minkowitz
(Ph.D., Columbia University)
Department of Special Education
Erasmus Hall High School
Brooklyn, New York

Illustratio
Michael K

D1444063

Research & Education Association

MAXnotes ® for
BILLY BUDD

Printed in the United States of America

Library of Congress Catalog Card Number 95-72134

International Standard Book Number 0-87891-007-7

MAXnotes ® is a registered trademark of
Research & Education Association, Piscataway, New Jersey 08854

What **MAXnotes®** *Will Do for You*

This book is intended to help you absorb the essential contents and features of Herman Melville's *Billy Budd* and to help you gain a thorough understanding of the work. The book has been designed to do this more quickly and effectively than any other study guide.

For best results, this **MAXnotes** book should be used as a companion to the actual work, not instead of it. The interaction between the two will greatly benefit you.

To help you in your studies, this book presents the most up-to-date interpretations of every section of the actual work, followed by questions and fully explained answers that will enable you to analyze the material critically. The questions also will help you to test your understanding of the work and will prepare you for discussions and exams.

Meaningful illustrations are included to further enhance your understanding and enjoyment of the literary work. The illustrations are designed to place you into the mood and spirit of the work's settings.

The **MAXnotes** also include summaries, character lists, explanations of plot, and section-by-section analyses. A biography of the author and discussion of the work's historical context will help you put this literary piece into the proper perspective of what is taking place.

The use of this study guide will save you the hours of preparation time that would ordinarily be required to arrive at a complete grasp of this work of literature. You will be well-prepared for classroom discussions, homework, and exams. The guidelines that are included for writing papers and reports on various topics will prepare you for any added work which may be assigned.

The **MAXnotes** will take your grades "to the max."

Dr. Max Fogiel
Program Director

Contents

**Each chapter includes List of Characters,
Summary, Analysis, Study Questions and
Answers, and Suggested Essay Topics.**

Introduction

The Life and Work of Herman Melville

Herman Melville was born in New York in 1819. His forebears were well-to-do and socially prominent, but his immediate family suffered from financial instability. His once prosperous household fell upon hard times. In 1832 his father's bankruptcy and death cut short his formal education and forced him to give up hopes for a suitable career. He tried several jobs to help out his family, including teaching school and clerking in a bank. In 1839, when all his attempts to restore his family's fortune had failed, Melville went to sea on a British ship, the *St. Lawrence*, bound for Liverpool.

In 1841 he signed aboard the *Achushnet*, which was headed for the South Seas. The brutal conditions aboard that ship led Melville and a companion to desert in the Marquesas Islands, where, in 1842, he became the well-treated captive of the cannibalistic Typees. Later he was rescued, only to become involved in a mutiny before finally returning home to the United States on a naval vessel in 1844.

Although he had never before considered a career as a writer, his friends urged him to publish memoirs of his adventures. His early works were quite successful, but his later writings were neither commercial successes nor critically appreciated. His successful sea novels included *Typee* (1846), *Omoo* (1847), *Redburn* (1848), and *White Jacket* (1850). In 1851, he wrote *Moby-Dick*, which most reviewers at the time criticized as incomprehensible.

After his story *Pierre* (1852) was similarly attacked, he began writing for magazines, and tried farming to make ends meet. He had married Elizabeth Shaw of Massachusetts in 1847, and he had a family to support. He tried his hand unsuccessfully at lecturing before finally taking a job as a customs inspector, a position he held for 20 years. He died on September 28, 1891, and lies buried in Woodlawn Cemetery in New York.

Historical Background

Herman Melville's life spanned a good part of the nineteenth century, a time of growth, upheaval, and change in the United States. It was a period during which the United States began to take its place among the world powers. In addition to the remarkable expansion of industry, there were equally outstanding developments in the fields of science, politics, and philosophy. The great intellectuals and literary figures of the day included William James, Walt Whitman, and England's Charles Darwin. Melville's literary idol was the great novelist Nathaniel Hawthorne, with whom Melville shared an emerging symbolist style of writing.

The abolition of slavery and the rise of trade unionism provoked a major rethinking of moral and social ideas. Many Americans were concerned with relieving the worst aspects of urban poverty. Some were influenced by the social ideas of transcendental philosophers Ralph Waldo Emerson and Henry David Thoreau as well as by the ideology of Karl Marx, who championed the rights of workers. The compelling ideas of his day, which are reflected in the themes of *Billy Budd*, included naturalism, the "noble savage," and idyllic innocence.

In his preface, Melville historically situates *Billy Budd* in the year 1797, the end of the eighteenth century, which has come to be called the "Age of Revolution." The upheavals that took place then were the forerunners of the changes in Melville's own time.

The eighteenth century saw the toppling of the old regimes throughout Europe. This heady atmosphere contributed to the Spithead and Nore mutinies in 1797, when ordinary seamen revolted against the British naval authorities to protest long-standing abuses. The mutinies greatly embarrassed Britain, and the ringleaders of the mutinies were swiftly and publicly executed. The need for swift justice in this context lies at the very heart of the crisis in *Billy Budd*.

Herman Melville often heard a family tale of how his older brother had presided over the court martial of an insubordinate sailor. It is very likely that Melville drew upon that tale, as well as upon his own experience with mutiny, for the development of *Billy Budd*.

In his later years, Melville was regarded as an avant-garde nonconformist, who was more widely known for having lived among cannibals than for his literary accomplishments. Neglected by the public, he died virtually forgotten.

At his death, Melville left a semi-final draft of *Billy Budd*. It remained unpublished until 1924, when there was a revival of interest in Melville's work.

Today Herman Melville is regarded as one of the greatest of all American writers. He is revered for his contribution to the creation of a characteristically American style of symbolic fiction.

Master List of Characters

Albert—*Captain Vere's hammock-boy on the* Indomitable.

The Armorer and the Captain of the Hold—*minor officers on board the* Indomitable.

Billy Budd—*an example of a "Handsome Sailor," a "jewel" pressed into service on the HMS* Indomitable.

Captain Graveling—*the skipper of the* Rights-of-Man, *who is reluctant to lose Billy to Lieutenant Radcliffe.*

Captain of the Marines, the First Lieutenant, and the Sailing Master—*the three members of the drumhead court that tries Billy for murder and mutiny.*

Captain Vere—*the virtuous commander of the* Indomitable, *who looks upon Billy as a son.*

Chaplain—*he tries to minister to Billy after the court martial.*

Dansker—*an old sailor to whom Billy turns for advice.*

Handsome Sailor—*a traditional figure exemplifying a specific type, a man who possesses natural goodness.*

John Claggart—*master-at-arms of the* Indomitable, *a sort of chief of police on board ship. He has a bad reputation and an unexplainable dislike of Billy.*

Purser—*in a digression, he discusses with the surgeon the strange phenomenon that occurs at Billy's death.*

Lieutenant Radcliffe—*he takes Billy off the* Rights-of-Man, *and presses him into service on the* Indomitable.

The Surgeon—*the medical officer on the* Indomitable *who pronounces Claggart dead.*

Summary of the Novella

Billy Budd typifies the Handsome Sailor in his demeanor of moral goodness and grace. A merchant seaman on the vessel the *Rights-of-Man*, he is removed from his ship by Lieutenant Radcliffe and pressed into service on board a British naval ship, the *Indomitable*. (Several versions, including the *Penguin Classics* series, name the ship the *Bellipotent* instead of the *Indomitable*.)

There he becomes a popular hero among his new shipmates, universally well-liked and respected by all with the exception of the sinister master-at-arms, John Claggart. Billy even becomes a favorite of Captain Vere, the commander of the *Indomitable*.

Claggart wrongfully accuses Billy Budd of participating in a mutiny plot and demands that Billy answer to the charge. Billy is unable to defend himself verbally because of a stammer. In angry frustration Billy suddenly strikes out at Claggart, stabbing him to death.

It is Captain Vere's sad duty to try Billy on the charges of murder and mutiny. Despite his love for Billy, Vere's first obligation is to the preservation of law and order.

Billy Budd is convicted by a drumhead court and sentenced to death. All hands on board are summoned to watch the sentence carried out. As Billy is hanged, his last words are "God Bless Captain Vere."

Despite the fact that officially Billy is found to be guilty, his shipmates remember him as a perfect example of moral goodness and innocence. His story becomes legend among sailors, even being immortalized in a ballad, "Billy in the Darbies."

Estimated Reading Time

Billy Budd is a novella (a short novel). Reading time is approximately 20 pages an hour. The novella has 105 pages, so it can be finished within four to five hours.

Billy Budd

Chapter 1

New Characters:

The Handsome Sailor: *a prototype of the morally good man, whose inner goodness is manifested by recognizable grace and charm*

Billy Budd: *a young seaman, an example of a Handsome Sailor*

Lieutenant Radcliffe: *boarding officer from the naval ship the* Indomitable

Captain Graveling: *shipmaster of the merchant vessel* Rights-of-Man

Summary

Melville describes the Handsome Sailor, a superior figure with both moral and physical strength and beauty. He digresses to describe an encounter with a common seaman who typifies the Handsome Sailor. This seaman is an African, who is clearly the leader and the center of attention as he romps along with his shipmates.

Such a celebrity too is Billy Budd, a foretopman of the British fleet during the last decade of the eighteenth century. He enters the King's Service after being removed from the merchant ship the *Rights-of-Man*, and forcibly taken aboard the HMS *Indomitable* by its boarding officer, Lieutenant Radcliffe. Billy accepts the impressment with good grace.

His shipmaster, Captain Graveling, is deeply troubled about

losing Billy. Graveling tells Radcliffe how Billy had sweetened the "sour ones," changed the tempers of the crew, and improved the relationships among them. Graveling doesn't want to lose his "peacemaker."

Graveling relates how one of the men, Red Whiskers, seemed to envy Billy and consequently kept harassing him, but Billy "forebore with him and reasoned with him...." One day Red Whiskers gave Billy a "dig in the ribs." Billy immediately "let fly his arm," much to Red Whiskers' astonishment. Afterward, Red Whiskers came to love Billy like all the rest of the crew.

Graveling's protests to Radcliffe fell on deaf ears. Radcliffe too recognizes Billy's special qualities, which will be equally beneficial to the *Indomitable.*

As Billy steps into the dinghy that will take him from the *Rights-of-Man* to the *Indomitable,* he waves his hat to bid good-bye to his former shipmates. Then, to the amusement of Lieutenant Radcliffe, Billy breaches "naval decorum" by saluting farewell to the ship itself.

Billy is compliant and accepting about the change in his life. He may even be looking forward to whatever new adventures await him on board the *Indomitable.*

Billy is assigned to the starboard watch as foretopman. He soon feels "at home" in his new service, and once again his good looks and geniality win him admiration and affection from his shipmates.

Whereas some of the other sailors are inclined to be sad after the day's work, Billy is uniformly cheerful. The others may have thoughts and concerns about wives, children, and other kin, but Billy has no family—"his entire family was practically invested in himself."

Analysis

The figure of the Handsome Sailor represents the forces of Goodness, which are manifested in the character of Billy Budd. In this first chapter, the emphasis upon Billy's naive innocence and natural decency foreshadows the conflict between Good and Evil which is a major theme of this story.

Foreshadowing appears again where we see that Billy's innocence does not preclude an artlessly violent reaction to Red

Whisker's "dig in the ribs." This reflexive strike portends a more ominous result later in the story. Likewise, Billy's breach of naval decorum when he salutes good-bye to the *Rights-of-Man* demonstrates his youthful impulsivity, and foreshadows his later problems with naval authority.

The matter of authority is addressed again by the issue of impressment, as well as by the respective portrayals of Lieutenant Radcliffe and Captain Graveling. In time of war, it was legal for the British Navy to forcibly enlist men taken from merchant ships. Captain Graveling's protests against Billy's impressment are overridden by Radcliffe's greater authority—greater despite the fact that Graveling is shipmaster of his vessel, while Radcliffe is only a minor officer on the HMS *Indomitable*.

Melville uses simile and metaphor to enhance his descriptions. Standing atop the yardarm-end, the Handsome Sailor is pictured as "tossed up as by the horns of Taurus against the thunderous sky...," not simply standing passively at his watch. Captain Graveling is described as a "ploughman of the troubled waters," who has a "certain musical chime in his voice." In his ability to calm the tempers of his shipmates, Billy is likened to "a Catholic priest striking peace in an Irish shindy."

Melville makes use of irony in the naming of the merchant ship, the *Rights-of-Man*. The impressment of Billy, while apparently legal in time of war, was a violation of Billy's individual human rights.

The name of the *Indomitable* is also significant, for it properly describes the invincibility of a British naval war ship and, as well, reflects the stern and resolute character of its commander, Captain Edward Fairfax Vere, who will be introduced in Chapter 6.

Study Questions

1. What are the qualities of a Handsome Sailor?
2. How does Billy exemplify the Handsome Sailor?
3. Explain the fact that Lieutenant Radcliffe appears to have greater authority than Captain Graveling.
4. Why is Captain Graveling sorry to lose Billy?
5. Describe what type of man Captain Graveling is.

6. Why does Billy offer no resistance to his impressment?

7. What is the reaction of Billy's shipmates when Billy is removed from the *Rights-of-Man*?

8. How does Billy bid farewell to his old life on the *Rights-of-Man*?

9. What is Lieutenant Radcliffe's reaction to the way Billy bids farewell?

10. How does Billy adjust to life on his new ship, the *Indomitable*?

Answers

1. The Handsome Sailor is naively good, honest, noble, congenial, open-hearted, graceful, and amiable. He also possesses great physical and moral strength.

2. Billy Budd is a natural peacemaker, well-loved by his shipmates, handsome, kind, and naively innocent.

3. Radcliffe is an officer of the British Navy, while Graveling is the skipper of a private merchant ship.

4. Graveling regards Billy as his "jewel," who changed the atmosphere aboard his ship from strife to comradely peace.

5. Captain Graveling is conscientious, prudent, and serious about his duties. He is a "respectable man."

6. Billy is a simple fatalist, open to whatever adventures lie in store for him.

7. Billy's shipmates are surprised and reproachful at Billy's willingness to leave, and they are saddened as well.

8. Billy waves his hat to his shipmates and salutes the ship itself.

9. Radcliffe is good-natured about this breach of decorum, but he wonders if Billy is making a "sly slur."

10. Billy is soon "at home on the *Indomitable*," where he is well-liked by his new mates for his congeniality.

Suggested Essay Topics

1.   Discuss the ethics of impressment during wartime. Consider
     the conflicting rights of the nation and the individual. Com-
     pare this issue with dilemmas of Melville's own era—for
     example, the problem of slavery with respect to the com-
     mercial interests of the southern farmers vs. the individual
     human rights of the slaves.

2.   Compare and contrast the characterizations of Captain
     Graveling and Lieutenant Radcliffe. Which of the two would
     you prefer to have as your superior officer? Why?

Chapter 2

Summary

     Billy very soon becomes a celebrity, as well as a favorite, among
the men aboard the *Indomitable*.

     Billy Budd is a very young man, and he looks even younger
than his years. His extremely youthful appearance is due largely to
his facial aspect, which Melville describes as that of "a lingering
adolescent." It is Billy's naiveté which is apparent in his face. Billy
also possesses a complexion so soft that it is "all but feminine in
(its natural) purity...."

     After Billy is taken aboard the *Indomitable*, he adapts extremely
well to life aboard ship, and he is liked by the crew. His striking
good looks have a favorable effect upon the common sailors as well
as upon the "more intelligent gentlemen of the quarter-deck." Billy,
however, takes little notice of his effect on people.

     Billy confides to his new shipmates that he is a foundling and
that he knows nothing of his origins. He seems to possess some
features that hint of noble descent. His intelligence is average, and
he has an obviously sound mind. Nevertheless, Billy is illiterate.
He does have the ability to compose his own songs, which he can
sing with a very charming voice.

     Despite his unblemished beauty, Billy has one flaw, "an occa-
sional liability to a vocal defect." In periods of stress, he often develops a stutter.

Analysis

In this chapter, Melville cites the Bible in several passages. Billy is much like Adam before "the urbane Serpent wriggled himself into his company." His virtuous innocence is pristine and unadulterated, deriving from "a period prior to Cain's city and citified man." The biblical references underscore the theme of conflict between Good and Evil that is constant throughout the story. These particular references also demonstrate that Billy is in many respects a "Noble Savage."

The description of Billy Budd's speech impediment foreshadows the dire events which will occur in Chapter 20. It is precisely this tragic flaw which will lead directly to Billy's downfall.

Melville makes extensive use of simile in these chapters. Billy's position aboard the *Indomitable* "is analogous to that of a rustic beauty transplanted from the provinces and brought into competition with the high-born dames of the court." A more modern analogy might be to the home-town beauty queen who is brought to the big city which is full of sophisticated and glamorous *femme fatales*. Melville's point is that Billy could more than "hold his own," even in such company.

Although Billy has "masculine beauty," he is "like the beautiful woman in one of Hawthorne's minor tales" who has but one blemish. (In Billy's case, the blemish is a vocal defect.)

The Nore mutiny is "analogous to the…irruption of contagious fever in a frame constitutionally sound…."

The use of simile is also seen in Melville's biblical references, where Billy is likened to Adam. Like Adam before the Fall, Billy Budd is a naturally moral man, a man of simple, youthful innocence.

Study Questions

1. How is Billy received by his new crew mates aboard the *Indomitable*?
2. What is the mystery concerning Billy's birth and origins?
3. How is Billy like Adam before the Fall?
4. What is Billy's one blemish?
5. How do Melville's references to Adam and the Serpent relate to the theme of conflict between Good and Evil?

6. What is the reaction of the "more intelligent gentlemen of the quarter-deck" to Billy's good looks?

7. To what classical hero does Melville compare Billy Budd?

8. What is the state of Billy's mental faculties?

9. How is Billy similar to other sailors?

10. How does Melville demonstrate that Billy Budd is not a "conventional" hero?

Answers

1. Billy is well-received by his new crew mates, and he has a favorable effect upon them.

2. Billy has a noble bearing, despite his humble condition; he explains that he is a foundling and doesn't know his own origins.

3. Like Adam, Billy is pristinely innocent and guileless.

4. In periods of emotional stress, Billy stutters.

5. The Bible story of Adam and his temptation is the prototype in Western civilization for the theme of conflict between Good and Evil.

6. These gentlemen greatly admire Billy for being a fine example of a pure Saxon strain of Englishman.

7. Melville compares Billy to the legendary Greek hero Hercules.

8. Despite being illiterate, Billy obviously is intelligent.

9. According to Melville, most sailors have simple, open natures.

10. Billy is not a conventional hero because of his simple innocence and naivete.

Suggested Essay Topics

1. Billy is likened to Adam before the Fall. What do you know of the Bible story of the Fall of Adam? Do you agree or disagree with Melville's assessment?

2. Billy is a foundling—from the clues in the story, imagine who his parents might have been. What is Billy's ethnic heritage? His religious heritage? The socioeconomic class of his forebears?

Chapter 3

Summary

At the time of Billy Budd's impressment, the *Indomitable* is on her way to join the Mediterranean fleet. The meeting with the fleet is accomplished shortly afterward.

Melville provides the historical context for Billy's impressment. This occurred in the same year, 1797, as did the mutinies at Spithead and Nore. The latter insurrection came to be called the "Great Mutiny," and it has gone down in British naval history as an event of dire threat to England.

After the Spithead mutiny was put down, some of the seamen's minor grievances were redressed, but these were not rectified sufficiently to prevent the later uprising at the Nore.

Not long afterward the mutineers were among the sailors who helped Lord Horatio Nelson win his victory at Trafalgar. This service seemed a full-fledged absolution for their previous mutinous behavior.

Analysis

Noting that Billy Budd's forced enlistment occurs as the ship is en route to join the Mediterranean fleet, Melville foreshadows the events which will occur when the *Indomitable* is again separated from the fleet. It is then that the fateful episode, which is at the heart of the story, takes place.

Melville mentions at the beginning of this chapter that the *Indomitable* customarily participates in maneuvers with the entire fleet. However, on certain rare occasions the *Indomitable* is used for special services that require a ship with superior sailing qualities, as well as a skipper who can act decisively when required to do so.

The Spithead and Nore mutinies which are spoken of in Chapter 3 foreshadow the pivotal events which appear later in the story. This context is crucial to the disposition of the commanding officer who will hold Billy's fate in his hands.

The basic obedience of the ordinary sailor is mentioned by Melville several times during this story. This obedience is seen in this chapter in the willingness to fight with patriotic fervor at the Trafalgar engagement by the men who had previously been mutineers.

We are thus given to understand that this character trait will prove significant to the unfolding of the story.

Study Questions

1. Where was the *Indomitable* en route to at the time of Billy's impressment?

2. In what year did the Spithead and Nore uprisings occur?

3. Which of the uprisings came to be known as the "Great Mutiny"?

4. Why was the "Great Mutiny" shaded "off into the historical background"?

5. After Spithead, why did the Nore mutiny occur?

6. How did the authorities finally put down the Nore mutiny?

7. Why weren't the mutinies more widespread among the rest of the British fleet?

8. How did many of the sailors involved in the mutinies absolve themselves of their crimes?

9. What was the cause for the uprisings?

10. How is the battle of Trafalgar remembered?

Answers

1. The *Indomitable* was en route to join the Mediterranean fleet.

2. The Spithead and Nore uprisings occurred in 1797.

3. The Nore uprising came to be known as the "Great Mutiny."

4. It was given little historical emphasis due to national pride.

5. The sailors' demands were not met after the Spithead uprising.

6. "Final suppression" was made possible by the loyalty of the marine corps and "voluntary resumption of loyalty" by the more influential leaders among the crew.

7. The mutinies were symptoms of troubles in a fleet that was "constitutionally sound."

8. Many of the mutineers were among the sailors who helped Nelson win his victories at the Nile and Trafalgar.

9. There were many practical grievances that ignited into a full-fledged uprising.

10. The battle of Trafalgar is remembered as a "scenic naval display," exemplified by "heroic magnificence."

Suggested Essay Topics

1. Discuss the events of 1797 and try to understand what the mood may have been among the British naval authorities in the aftermath of the mutinies.

2. Discuss Melville's analogy: "To some extent the Nore Mutiny may be regarded as analogous to the distempering irruption of contagious fever in a frame constitutionally sound, and which anon throws it off." Explain what Melville means. Discuss whether or not the analogy helps you to understand the Nore Mutiny.

Chapters 4–5

New Character:

Lord Horatio Nelson: *A great naval hero, immortalized by the poet Alfred Tennyson as "the greatest sailor since the world began"*

Summary

Digressing in Chapter 4, Melville speaks about the invention of gunpowder and the revolution in warfare this development has brought about. He regrets the fact that firearms make possible the ability to kill at a distance. Melville regards this distancing as a cowardly way to fight. Previously, warfare at sea had been largely "crossing steel with steel."

Nevertheless, despite the use of firearms, there is one Great Sailor, Lord Nelson, who still exhibits the traits of bravery and poise in battle. Melville praises Nelson for having fought valiantly aboard the *Victory*, although he notes that some critics have faulted Nelson for excessive self-exposure during the battle. These same critics sometimes add that Nelson was likewise foolhardy at Trafalgar, and that had he been more cautious, he might have survived that battle. Had he lived, Nelson might have been able to prevent the excessive loss of life that occurred as a result of a rather inept second in command.

In opposition to those critics, however, Melville believes that Nelson was the model of "the great sailor," and that his bravery was motivated by an abiding sense of duty. He mentions that Nelson was accorded many honors for his service to the crown.

On the eve before the fatal battle at Trafalgar was to take place, Lord Nelson sat down to write his last will and testament, garbed in full dress and adorned with his medals. Melville acknowledges that this might prove the critics right with respect to Nelson's vanity. However, he approves Nelson's pride under those circumstances. He remarks that Nelson's actions were the practical embodiment of the type of heroic sentiments written in verses by poets.

Much of the discontent that led to the two mutinies continued to exist long afterward. While Nelson was still vice admiral, he was directed by the admiral to shift his command from the *Captain* to the *Theseus* in order to win back the crew, "by force of his mere presence," to an allegiance to the British Navy.

One of the grievances that continued unabated after the mutinies was the practice of impressment. Melville notes that its repeal would have crippled the fleet. The many different battlefronts required an insatiable demand for sailors.

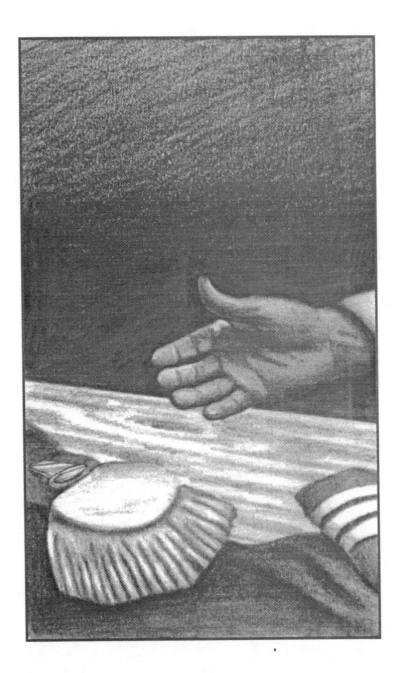

Analysis

Melville's digression about the changes in warfare due to the invention of gunpowder sets the stage for his introduction of Lord Horatio Nelson, the quintessential maritime hero, a man driven by a strong moral sense of duty and possessing strong leadership qualities. Nelson's role in the aftermath of the mutinies is given a great deal of emphasis.

Melville's extensive reference to Lord Horatio Nelson prefigures the introduction of Captain Vere in Chapter 6. Like Nelson, Captain Vere will prove to have superior moral qualities and leadership skills which will be needed in extraordinary circumstances.

The fact that not every grievance was redressed after the mutinies sets up the context for suspicion and distrust, and for the dire events that will follow.

Study Questions

1. Who was Lord Horatio Nelson?

2. Why has Nelson come to be known as "the Great Sailor"?

3. Which grievance of the mutineers was *not* redressed after the mutinies?

4. Why was impressment still widely practiced after the mutinies?

5. Why was Lord Nelson directed by the admiral to take command of the *Theseus*?

6. How did Nelson deal with the crew of the *Theseus*?

7. Which grievances at the Spithead and Nore were redressed after the mutinies?

8. Who referred to Lord Nelson as the "greatest sailor since our world began"?

9. In the aftermath of the mutinies, how did some British officers ensure the loyalty of their men in battle?

10. Why was "precautionary vigilance" practiced at sea?

Answers

1. Lord Horatio Nelson was considered the greatest British naval hero.

2. Nelson was known as "the Great Sailor" because of his bravery and moral leadership qualities.

3. Impressment was still widely used as a way to enlist a crew.

4. The naval authorities believed there was no other way to ensure a fully manned crew.

5. The crew of the *Theseus* exhibited signs of discontent, and it was believed that Nelson had the qualities that could calm the tempers of the men.

6. Nelson won them over by force of his presence.

7. The problems of shoddy cloth and unsound rations were resolved in the aftermath of the mutinies.

8. Alfred Tennyson, in his funeral oration, called Nelson "the greatest sailor since our world began."

9. In some instances they stood "with drawn swords" to ensure that the crew manned the guns during battle.

10. Precautionary vigilance was needed since there was always the concern that an uprising could begin anew.

Suggested Essay Topics

1. Billy is the "Handsome Sailor" and Lord Nelson is the "Great Sailor." Explain the distinction between a "Handsome Sailor" and a "Great Sailor."

2. Imagine that you are a young officer on board a British maritime ship in the aftermath of the Spithead and Nore uprisings. Can you trust the crew? How do you feel if you have to "stand with drawn sword" to make sure the crew will fight in battle?

Chapters 6–8

New Characters:

Captain Edward Fairfax Vere: *the virtuous commander of the* Indomitable

John Claggart: *master-at-arms on board the* Indomitable, *who has a mysterious and disreputable past*

Summary

The casual observer of the crew and the activity on board the *Indomitable* will find little evidence of the discontent and the mutinies spoken of in previous chapters. The commissioned officers behave with equanimity toward the crew. In this they take their cue from their superior officer, Captain the Honorable Edward Fairfax Vere.

Captain Vere is a "sailor of distinction," as well as a man of nobility. He is a conscientious leader, and an evenhanded, although strict disciplinarian. In contrast to his largely illiterate crew, Captain Vere is an ardent and voracious reader, with wide interests in many varied subjects of study.

At times Captain Vere has betrayed "a certain dreaminess of mood." A "favorite kinsman," having taken the phrase from some lines of poetry, has given him the pet name, "Starry Vere."

Vere possesses many talents and interests besides those pertaining to his naval command. He is a man of firm conviction, not easily swayed by popular opinion. Among his crew and peers he is well liked and respected, although he is not particularly companionable. He is considered undemonstrative and "dry and bookish."

John Claggart, the master-at-arms, is "sort of chief of police" aboard the *Indomitable*. At age 35, Claggart is tall, spare, and rather pallid of complexion, which seems to "hint of something defective or abnormal in the constitution and blood." He is apparently well educated, however, nothing is known of his former life. He might have been English by birth, although his speech has a bit of a foreign accent.

There is a rumor among the crew that John Claggart was once involved in a fraud, and that his sea duty is a result of his criminal

past. Indeed, at that time the British navy was known to welcome men who were fleeing from some scandal or other in civilian life.

When Claggart entered the service, he was assigned, as a novice, to "the least honorable section of a man-of-war's crew. " He quickly advanced to the position of master-at-arms.

Analysis

Despite pointing to Vere's many exemplary qualities, Melville also emphasizes his "settled convictions." Vere's rigid moral attitude will prove significant as the story progresses.

In Chapter 6, the reason for Melville's description of Lord Nelson in prior chapters becomes clear. We are induced to compare Nelson with Captain Vere, who possesses many of the same qualities of the "Great Sailor."

Another comparison that Melville implies here is between Billy Budd and John Claggart, both of whom have pasts shrouded in mystery. However, it is important to note that Claggart, unlike Billy, is extremely well educated and urbane as well.

Melville likens John Claggart to the infamous Reverend Titus Oates, a man who fomented anti-Catholic bias through false charges of an assassination plot against King Charles II. Melville is thus preparing the reader for the dire events caused by false charges which will come to pass in later chapters.

A further comparison is implied between the civilized morality of the cultured and educated Captain Vere and the pristine moral goodness of Billy Budd, the illiterate "Noble Savage." Both will display nobility of spirit in future chapters, but whereas Billy's character is purely natural, Vere's is tempered by the harsh demands of warfare in a "civilized" society.

Study Questions

1. What qualities does Captain Vere share with Lord Horatio Nelson?

2. How did Vere receive his nickname, "Starry Vere"?

3. Of what trait do Vere's men complain?

4. What is the major duty of the master-at-arms?

5. Describe John Claggart's physical appearance.

6. How does Claggart's appearance suggest his character and personality?

7. What is rumored about Claggart's past?

8. Why did the British navy accept the enlistment of men of disrepute?

9. How did Claggart manage to advance to the rank of master-at-arms?

10. What is the source of John Claggart's power and authority aboard the *Indomitable*?

Answers

1. They are both patriotic, valiant, noble, and superior moral leaders of men.

2. A relative extracted and applied these lines from a poem by Andrew Marvell:

   > "This 'tis to have been from the first
   > In a domestic heaven nursed,
   > Under the discipline severe
   > Of Fairfax and the starry Vere."

3. They complain that Vere is rigid and pedantic.

4. The chief duty of the master-at-arms is to preserve order on the gun decks.

5. Claggart is tall and thin. He is good-looking, but he has a rather heavy chin. He is pallid, and he has black, curly hair.

6. His pallor seems unhealthy or sinister to the men.

7. It is rumored that Claggart has a disreputable past, and that he had been involved in a criminal act.

8. When crewmen were desperately needed, the British navy was willing to accept any person, regardless of background.

9. Claggart advanced quickly through a combination of superior intelligence, hard work, and "ingratiating deference."

10. Claggart built a power base through the use of compliant underlings.

Suggested Essay Topics

1. Compare and contrast Billy Budd's background and situation with John Claggart's.

2. Defend or critique the policy of emptying prisons in order to man the British naval ships.

Chapters 9–11

New Character:

Dansker: *an old veteran aboard the* Indomitable *who befriends Billy Budd, and who tries to warn Billy to look out for John Claggart*

Summary

Billy is competent in his position as foretopman aboard the *Indomitable.*

When they are not busy working, Billy's topmates form a kind of "aerial club." They lounge around against the smaller sails where they relax, tell tales, and generally amuse themselves.

Billy is good-naturedly teased by his mates because he is conscientious about responding to calls to duty. His alertness to his obligations derives from having witnessed a formal gangway punishment. The culprit was whipped on his bare back and was deeply humiliated. Billy has resolved never to act in such a way as to merit such severe punishment. Nevertheless, he is astonished to find that occasionally he gets into some petty trouble. He cannot imagine, for example, how his hammock could be in such disarray that the result is a rebuke from one of the ship's corporals.

Billy becomes acquainted with Dansker, an old veteran who had previously served with Nelson aboard the *Agamemnon.* Dansker's nickname, "Board-her-in-the smoke," was earned when he was part of a boarding party from the *Agamemnon.* Dansker

was hit in the face by a shot, and he remains with a scar that resembles "a streak of dawn's light falling" across his dark-complexioned countenance.

Dansker's chief character trait is his "pithy, guarded cynicism." At first he is amused by Billy's incongruity aboard a naval warship. His initial amusement soon turns to affection and concern. Unlike the other junior members of the crew, Billy has always greeted Dansker with affectionate respect.

When Billy tells Dansker of his troubles, the latter warns him that "Jimmy Legs" (a derogatory name he is using to refer to the master-at-arms) is "down" on him. Billy is incredulous, for Claggart has always spoken kindly to him. Dansker tries to explain that it is precisely Claggart's show of kindness that is a sure sign he is indeed "down" on Billy.

The next day, when the ship is rolling from the wind, Billy's soup spills upon the newly scrubbed deck. Claggart happens to be passing at that moment. He appears to think nothing of it until he observes that it was Billy who had done the spilling. He is about to say something "hasty," when he thinks better of it and says playfully to Billy, "Handsomely done, my lad! And handsome is as handsome does." Everyone present takes the remark as humorous, and they laugh "with counterfeited glee." Billy is thus convinced that Dansker is wrong about Claggart being "down" on him.

But in fact, Claggart is indeed "down" on Billy Budd. This dislike is spontaneous and irrational. Perhaps it is due to the fact that the two personalities are wholly opposite: Billy is naturally wholesome and good, while Claggart appears to be naturally depraved.

Melville quotes Plato on "natural depravity," and explains that a naturally depraved person would not appear so obviously, that such a person would eschew "vices and small sins," and "partakes nothing of the sordid or sensational." Rather, such a person would be very serious, logical, and at the same time harbor an insane antipathy toward some special object. Claggart fits this description.

Analysis

In these chapters, the conflict between Good and Evil comes to the fore. Billy and John Claggart have parallel lives, yet totally divergent personalities. Both have mysterious pasts, and both exhibit indications of nobility. However, Billy has developed a naive and angelic disposition, in contrast to Claggart, who is sophisticated, cunning, and pernicious. It is typical of these two personality types that the former should be trusting of the latter, and that the latter should be suspicious and antagonistic toward the former.

In fact, it is clear that Claggart despises Billy precisely because the young sailor possesses virtues which he lacks—sincerity, integrity, and affability. Just as Claggart symbolizes all that is depraved and cruel in this world, Billy symbolizes uncorrupted, simple spirituality.

Despite Billy's trust, the reader is provided with clues that reveal Claggart is indeed "down" on him. Claggart's sudden attention to the spilled soup when he discovers the identity of the perpetrator, as well as the sarcasm in his remark, "handsome is as handsome does," disclose his hostility toward Billy. Further, in Chapter 11 we are made aware of the depths of corruption in Claggart's nature.

Melville uses metaphor when he speaks of Dansker as "the old Merlin." Merlin was both a seer and a confidant in King Arthur's Court, roles which Dansker takes with respect to Billy Budd. Metaphor is used again where Dansker is called "the old sea-Chiron." Like that mythological centaur, Dansker tries to be an instructing oracle and friend to Billy Budd, "his young Achilles." Achilles, a mythological figure noted for his bravery and strength, has one tragic flaw. It is his heel, a weak spot where he is mortally vulnerable. The term "Achille's heel" has come to denote a person's special deficiency or failing. We have already learned that Billy's Achille's heel is his stutter.

Study Questions

1. Why is Billy so meticulous about doing his duty on board ship?

2. How does Billy get into trouble with one of the ship's corporals?

3. Why does Billy seek out Dansker to ask for advice?

4. How did Dansker get his nickname, "Board-her-in-the-smoke"?

5. What is Dansker's first impression of Billy Budd?

6. Why does Dansker "take to" Billy?

7. What reason does Billy give Dansker for trusting in Claggart?

8. What is Claggart's reaction when he realizes Billy spilled the soup?

9. How are Billy Budd and John Claggart completely antithetical?

10. What does Melville mean by "natural depravity"?

Answers

1. Billy once observed the beating of a sailor who had been derelict in his duty.

2. Inexplicably, Billy's gear is in disarray.

3. Billy selected Dansker as a confidant because he was a wise and experienced old veteran.

4. Dansker's nickname derives from two sources: a scar on his "blue-peppered complexion," that looked like "a streak of dawn's light falling athwart the dark visage," as well as the boarding party incident at which the scar was incurred.

5. Dansker is amused by the incongruity of an innocent among the rough and experienced seamen.

6. Whereas most of the young sailors are repelled by the old man, Billy reveres him and greets him with respect.

7. Billy says that Claggart has always spoken kindly to him.

8. His first impulse is to say something harsh, but instead he makes a sarcastically humorous remark.

9. Billy is naive, trusting, and naturally good. Claggart is sophisticated, suspicious, and naturally depraved.

10. A depravity that is inherent to the person, characterized by evil that "Folds itself into the cloak of respectability."

Suggested Essay Topics

1. Read these lines written by Thomas Brown in the seventeenth century:

    > I do not love thee Doctor Fell
    > The reason why I cannot tell
    > But this I know and know full well
    > I do not love thee Doctor Fell

    Explain how the sentiment in this poem relates to John Claggart's feelings toward Billy Budd, as well as to Melville's depiction of Claggart.

2. Could Dansker have done more to warn Billy Budd? Does he have a moral responsibility to protect Billy? State your position and provide three reasons for that position, based upon the text.

Chapters 12–14

New Character:

Squeak: *one of Claggart's "more cunning corporals," a spy and henchman for Claggart*

Summary

At the beginning of this chapter, Melville digresses a bit to note that there are certain criminal cases which seem to baffle the courts. The juries hear various legal and medical experts who disagree with one another, and the courts are thwarted in their search for separating falsity from truth. Melville suggests, "Why not subpoena as well the clerical proficients?" He argues that the clerics come into contact with human beings during their most unguarded moments, and that they, rather than the medical or legal professionals, are more likely to truly know what is in the human heart.

John Claggart is a fine-looking man, who is neat and careful in his dress. Despite his own good looks, Claggart cannot compete with Billy Budd's extraordinary male beauty. By his remark, "Handsome is as handsome does," Claggart has revealed the source of his antagonism toward Billy: it is envy of his "significant personal beauty."

Although envy and antipathy seem to be irreconcilable traits, according to human reason, in actual human emotion the two very often appear as co-joined twins. Envy is a fervent emotion, and no amount of intelligence can safeguard a man from it.

Melville points out that it is not simply crude envy that motivates Claggart, who is both charmed and repelled by Billy.

Claggart is powerless to "annul the elemental evil." Like "the scorpion for which the Creator alone is responsible," he must act out his destiny.

Claggart assumes that Billy's spilling of the soup was deliberate as a "sly escape" for a reciprocal feeling of antipathy. This incident confirms for Claggart certain reports brought to him by "Squeak," one of his corporals.

Squeak has been getting Billy into trouble by messing up his gear. He understands that Claggart hates Billy, and so takes it upon himself to "foment the ill blood" by inventing reports of Billy's wrongdoing. Claggart never checks Squeak's reports, and he is more than willing to believe the worst of Billy Budd.

Like all of us, Claggart has a conscience, but his desire and need to find Billy blameworthy subvert his conscience.

Analysis

In Chapter 12, Melville digresses to suggest that members of the clergy would be better experts than lawyers or medical men since they understand the evils of the human heart. He mentions the "mysteries of iniquity," a biblical reference (2 Thess. 2:7) to the promise of the second coming of Christ, who will establish justice.

Claggart's nature is compared to that of the scorpion which, however destructive, is God's creature destined to act in a scorpion-like way to bring about God's mysterious will. Like the scorpion, Claggart cannot help but be what he is.

Another biblical reference here is the contrast between Claggart's envy of Billy and the brooding envy Saul felt toward David. King Saul deeply loved the young shepherd who could sooth and charm him with his music, but when David's popularity among

the people surpassed Saul's, his love turned to rivalry and malice. However, Melville notes that Claggart's envy "struck deeper."

Melville attempts to explain Claggart's evil nature by referring to a well-known case of Siamese twins, Chang and Eng. Like that conjoined pair, envy and antipathy are very often inseparable in the human heart, despite their logical disunity.

What is more, Claggart cannot imagine that his malice toward Billy is unreciprocated. This is how Claggart assuages his conscience, which, despite his depravity, he must answer to like all other human beings. His need and desire to find Billy blameworthy subvert and blind his conscience.

The character "Squeak" is aptly named. The name implies a squealer, who would "rat" on a shipmate in order to ingratiate himself with his superior.

Study Questions

1. Why does Melville suggest that clerics would be good experts in a court of law?

2. According to Melville, how are envy and antipathy related?

3. What quality of Billy's has served to move Claggart against him?

4. How is Claggart's envy different from the envy of Saul for David?

5. How is Claggart like the scorpion?

6. What is the reason for Claggart's reaction to the spilled soup?

7. Why does Squeak make up charges against Billy?

8. Why doesn't Claggart check on Squeak's reports?

9. How does Squeak's name reflect his personality?

10. How does Claggart manage to override his conscience?

Answers

1. According to Melville, clerics have better insight into the human heart.

2. Envy and antipathy are like conjoined twins.

3. Billy's physical beauty has been the initial motive for Claggart's antipathy.

4. Claggart's envy is more profound than Saul's.

5. Like the scorpion, Claggart has been created by God to fulfill a certain destiny.

6. Claggart imagines that Billy has deliberately spilled the soup to express his own dislike of Claggart.

7. Squeak perceives Claggart's dislike of Billy, and he wishes to ingratiate himself.

8. Claggart prefers to believe ill of Billy, so he takes Squeak's reports at face value.

9. "Squeak" implies a rat, and Squeak "rats" on Billy to Claggart.

10. Claggart prefers to think ill of Billy so he can rationalize that he is justified to have animosity toward him.

Suggested Essay Topics

1. Can Squeak's actions be defended or are they indefensible? Take a position and argue for that position based upon what you know about the characters from the text.

2. Do you agree or disagree that, like the scorpion, Claggart cannot help but be what he is. Consider the following—are our personalities inborn, or can we change them? Can upbringing and education affect our personalities? What about destiny—does God make us the way we are for some inexplicable reason? What is Melville's position? What was the popular notion about predestination in Melville's own time?

Chapters 15–18

New Characters:

The Afterguardsman: *a mysterious figure who tries to inveigle Billy into participating in a mutinous intrigue*

Red Pepper: *a forecastleman who asks Billy about the commotion in the forechains*

The Armorer and the Captain of the Hold: *two minor officers who begin to take note of Billy*

Summary

A few days after the spilled soup incident, an even more troubling event occurs.

Billy is awakened from sleep by a touch and a "quick whisper," by a shadowed person whom Billy cannot discern. He is instructed to go to the sheltered forechains, for "there is something in the wind." Loath to say "no" to anyone, Billy does as he is told.

He is met in the forechains by someone whose face he cannot distinguish in the darkness. However, from his "outline and carriage" Billy believes he is one of the afterguardsmen. The mysterious stranger tells Billy that there's a "gang of us," among the sailors who have been impressed. He holds up two small shiny objects that look like guineas, and he appears to offer them to Billy.

Billy grasps that something unsavory and mutinous is being proposed, and in his anxiety, he begins to stutter. When he threatens to toss the mysterious person over the rail, the man quickly disappears into the shadows.

The noisy rendezvous has awakened a forecastleman, Red Pepper, who recognizes Billy's stutter. When questioned by Red Pepper, he is able to master "the impediment." Billy makes light of the incident, saying merely that he found the afterguardsman in "our part of the ship." The explanation satisfies Red Pepper, for sailors are typically jealous of any territorial infringements.

Despite making light of the incident, Billy is disturbed and confounded by the strange occurrence. It is the first time in his life that he has been approached in so underhanded a fashion. He wonders what it all means, and he wonders whether or not the shiny objects shown to him were really gold coins. The more he reflects upon the incident, the more troubled he becomes.

The next afternoon Billy sees the afterguardsman, who nods in recognition. A few days later, he again greets Billy in a friendly manner. Although Billy is extremely upset, it doesn't occur to him that he might have a duty to report the overture "in the proper quarter."

He unburdens himself to Dansker, who says that the after-guardsman is merely a "cats-paw," that is, a dupe for the machinations of the master-at-arms. Billy cannot believe that a man who "always had a kind word for him" can be so duplicitous.

In fact, Claggart seems friendlier to Billy than ever before. He is polite and amiable to Billy, but when he comes upon him suddenly, a peculiar "red light" appears to emanate from his eyes. Billy notices that the master-at-arms behaves "rather queer at times," but thinks little of it.

Thus, despite Dansker's advice, Billy remains child-like in his understanding of John Claggart's true feelings toward him. It is not that Billy is unintelligent, but rather that he is simple-minded. In fact, Melville, points out, simple-mindedness is a characteristic of sailors, who are "a juvenile race." He suggests that this simple-mindedness is a direct result of being trained to blind obedience, rather than trained to think for themselves.

After the incident Billy finds several unusual things occurring. First, he is no longer getting into the kinds of petty trouble as he was previously. Second, the armorer and the captain of the hold begin to take note of Billy and they act as though they have been told something unflattering about him.

Analysis

Billy's stuttered threat in reply to the mutinous proposal offered by the afterguardsman is another incident which foreshadows the tragic response to a moral peril.

Claggart is able to engage others (for example, the afterguardsman, the armorer, and the captain of the hold) in his plot against Billy. Dansker suggests that the afterguardsman has been duped by Claggart. The same is very likely the case with the armorer and the captain of the hold, since they are Claggart's "messmates...with ears convenient to his confidential tongue."

Melville points out that sailors are accustomed to obeying orders. This reliance on external governance prevents the maturation of critical thinking and leads to inflexible and stereotypical behavior. This will prove significant for the tragedy that will unfold.

It is Billy's very goodness that will lead to his downfall. "Innocence was his blinder," Melville tells us. Although he understands what the afterguardsman is up to, Billy is too unsophisticated to believe that Claggart could be plotting against him. Moreover, his "novice-magnanimity" precludes him from taking the only step that can protect him from the peril that will befall him. He is afraid of being considered a "tell-tale," so he will not report the matter to the authorities.

Melville again takes note of Claggart's contradictory feelings toward Billy. The master-at-arms' pensive expression when he looks at Billy appears to contain a "soft yearning," as though Claggart could have loved Billy dearly if not for his fated abhorrence of him.

Study Questions

1. What is Billy's reaction to being summoned out of his sleep to a secret meeting?

2. What is Billy's response to the afterguardsman's offer?

3. What explanation does Billy give to Red Pepper?

4. Why is Billy disturbed by the incident?

5. What is Dansker's explanation for the strange happenings?

6. How does Billy react to Dansker's interpretation?

7. Why doesn't Dansker give Billy more specific advice?

8. Why doesn't Billy report the afterguardsman to the proper authorities?

9. How does Claggart react to Billy during this period?

10. How does Claggart disguise his "monomania," that is, his obsession with Billy?

Answers

1. Billy does as he is told and goes to meet the stranger.

2. He is resentful and angry, and he threatens to throw the afterguardsman over the rail.

3. He tells Red Pepper that he was angry because the afterguardsman was in the wrong part of the ship.

4. He is bewildered and upset because the intrigue was "disturbingly alien to him."

5. Dansker's explanation is that "Jimmy-Legs" is down on Billy Budd.

6. Billy refuses to believe that the master-at-arms could be plotting against him.

7. Dansker has learned from "long experience" that it is unwise to interfere or give advice to others.

8. Billy is trying to avoid doing the "dirty work of a tell-tale."

9. Claggart is obsessed with Billy, alternating between extreme feelings of hatred and yearning.

10. He covers up with his "self-contained and rational demeanor."

Suggested Essay Topics

1. Is innocence of character necessarily a virtue? How might Billy handle the afterguardsman's proposition if he were more worldly or sophisticated?

2. Describe the complexity of Claggart's feelings toward Billy. How might their relationship be different if Claggart were to follow his inclination to love instead of hate Billy?

Chapter 19

New Character:

Albert: *Captain Vere's hammock-boy who is sent to summon Billy Budd*

Summary

The *Indomitable* is occasionally detached from the squadron and used for special service. This is due to the esteem in which Captain Vere is held. He is known to possess the ability to adapt well to new situations, make quick decisions when necessary, and take charge under difficult circumstances.

During one such expedition, an enemy ship is sighted. It proves to be a warship. Although pursued by the *Indomitable*, the enemy flees and manages to escape.

During the return trip back to the fleet, the master-at-arms appears before Captain Vere. He stands waiting deferentially, hat in hand, waiting to be acknowledged by Vere. Vere has an inexplicable distaste for him. When he realizes who is standing before him, a "peculiar expression" comes upon Vere's face.

Claggart tells Captain Vere that during the chase he became convinced that one of the sailors is a "dangerous character," and that "something clandestine" is going on, "prompted by the sailor in question."

Captain Vere is not "unduly disturbed" by Claggart's accusation. He mistrusts Claggart. Vere demands that Claggart name the "dangerous man," and he is astonished when "William Budd" is named. Vere warns Claggart not to perjure himself, but he sticks to his story.

Vere prefers to avoid the undesirable effect of a full inquiry. He decides to have Claggart confront Billy in his presence. Vere directs Albert, his hammock-boy, to bring Billy to him.

Analysis

Melville repeats his comparison between Vere and Lord Horatio Nelson. Like Nelson in an earlier chapter, Captain Vere is often called upon for "any duty where...a prompt initiative might have to be taken" requiring his special abilities beyond "those qualities implied in good seamanship." Melville thus announces to the reader that such an event is about to occur.

Vere is not taken in by John Claggart, and he is skeptical about the latter's accusation. Nevertheless, his duty is to investigate the charges.

Claggart imputes to Billy Budd the very abominable traits which he himself possesses: he claims that Billy "insinuates himself into the goodwill of his shipmates."

Study Questions

1. Why was the *Indomitable* detached from the rest of the squadron?

2. How does Claggart approach Captain Vere?

3. What is Captain Vere's opinion of John Claggart?

4. What does Claggart tell Captain Vere about Billy Budd?

5. Why doesn't Captain Vere trust Claggart?

6. What does Captain Vere do in response to Claggart's accusation?

7. What character trait does Claggart impute to Billy Budd?

8. Why does Captain Vere proceed with caution?

9. How is Claggart's evil intent toward Billy revealed?

10. What is Vere's opinion of Billy Budd?

Answers

1. Due to a shortage of frigates in the British fleet, the *Indomitable* was detached from the squadron and sent on a special mission.

2. Claggart approaches Captain Vere with deference, cap in hand.

3. Although he doesn't know him well, he takes an inexplicable dislike to Claggart.

4. Claggart tells Captain Vere that Billy Budd is a dangerous man who is plotting something clandestine.

5. Claggart reminds Vere of a perjurer he once knew while participating in a court martial.

6. Captain Vere summons Billy in order to observe his reaction when Claggart accuses him to his face.

7. Claggart imputes to Billy the trait of duplicity.

8. Vere doesn't want to act hastily upon what he believes is false information.

9. By his contrived accusation, Claggart's plot against Billy is revealed.

10. Vere has a very high opinion of Billy.

Suggested Essay Topics

1. Captain Vere is skeptical about Claggart's accusation. What is Vere's opinion of Claggart? Substantiate your answer by citing the text.

2. What is the significance of Claggart's accusation coming while the *Indomitable* is detached from the rest of the fleet?

Chapters 20–21

New Character:

The Surgeon: *he is summoned after Billy knocks down John Claggart, and it is he who pronounces Claggart dead. Later, he discusses the mysterious occurrence at Billy's death*

Summary

At first, Billy is surprised but not at all apprehensive. Claggart approaches Billy, "mesmerically looking him in the eye," and repeats the accusation. Only slowly does Billy come to understand of what he is being accused, and he is transfixed. Vere urges him to "Speak, man...Speak! Defend yourself!" Horrified by the accusation, his stutter becomes intensified "into a convulsed tongue-tie." Straining to obey Vere's counsel to defend himself, Billy feels like he is suffocating.

Vere had not previously known about Billy's impediment, but now he surmises the problem and attempts to soothe Billy. However, his words have the opposite effect, for Billy responds by straining even harder to please. In his frustration, his right arm shoots out at Claggart, who falls to the deck. Captain Vere's manner changes from "the father in him" to "military disciplinarian." He sends Billy to a stateroom and orders him to remain there, while he sends Albert to summon the surgeon.

The surgeon confirms that Claggart is dead. He is disconcerted by Vere's appearance and is concerned for his mental stability.

Vere orders the surgeon to tell the lieutenants and the captain of the marines what has happened, and to instruct them to "keep the matter to themselves." The surgeon is to inform them, too, that there is to be a drumhead court.

The surgeon complies, although he is troubled by the Captain's decision. He feels it is "impolitic" to do so, and that a better course would be to wait until they could rejoin the squadron and refer the matter to the admiral.

Analysis

Claggart's appearance undergoes a startling change as he stands facing Billy with his accusations. His eyes turn from their normal blue to a muddy purple color, and the "lights of human intelligence" seem to go out. His face loses its human expression, and he takes on the appearance of an alien "uncatalogued creature of the deep." Melville thus dehumanizes Claggart, and he suggests that he has become a monster.

Billy's stutter, and his violent agony, have been foreshadowed by his response to the plotting afterguardsman, as well as by an earlier incident while still aboard the merchant ship, the *Rights-of-Man*.

Captain Vere's first reaction to Billy's act is to cry out, "Fated Boy...What have you done?..." Melville is indicating here the doctrine of predestination, which is derived not only from Greek mythology, but also from several Christian dogmas.

Vere's outcry that Claggart's death is "the divine judgment on Ananias" is a reference to Acts 5.1-9, which relates the swift and sudden punishment meted out to an early Christian who had conspired to cheat and lie. Vere proclaims that Claggart has been "Struck dead by an angel of God! Yet the angel must hang!" The reader is thus alerted to what will be Vere's position concerning justice for Billy's crime.

Claggart's death is caused by Claggart's evil intent as well as by Billy's childlike temper, his physical strength, his stammer, and his exceptional naivete. These traits were noted in previous chapters, foreshadowing the dire events in this chapter and in chapters to come.

Study Questions

1. What is Billy's first reaction to Claggart's accusation?

2. Why does Vere want to observe the confrontation between Claggart and Billy?

3. Why doesn't Billy Budd answer his accuser?

4. Since he cannot speak, what action does Billy take?

5. Why does Captain Vere send for the surgeon?

6. What does Captain Vere decide to do about the crime?

7. What is the surgeon's concern about Captain Vere?

8. What does the surgeon do?

9. What were the reactions of the lieutenants and the captain of the marines?

10. What is a "drumhead court"?

Answers

1. Billy is surprised but not apprehensive.

2. Vere wants to observe the expressions in each man's face.

3. In moments of stress Billy develops a speech impediment.

4. In frustration, Billy strikes out at Claggart and inadvertently kills him.

5. He wants to ascertain whether or not Claggart is dead.

6. Captain Vere decides to hold a drumhead court.

7. The surgeon is worried about Vere's mental health, and he also believes it is impolitic to hold a drumhead court.

8. The surgeon obeys the captain's orders and relates what has happened to the lieutenants and the captain of the marines.

9. Like the surgeon, they too would have preferred to wait for the admiral.

10. It is a court convened in the field rather than in a regular military courtroom.

Suggested Essay Topics

1. From the text, what do we know of Captain Vere's personality, and how can we expect him to handle Billy's trial?

2. How might the outcome have been different if Billy had been able to speak? Write a response that Billy might have made to Claggart's accusations.

3. How is *Billy Budd* like a Greek tragedy? What is the role of fate? What is Billy's tragic flaw?

Chapter 22

New Characters:

The First Lieutenant, the Captain of the Marines, and the Sailing Master: *these are the officers who are chosen by Captain Vere to compose the drumhead court*

Summary

There is a blurred line between sanity and insanity. Melville tells us that it is up to the reader to determine whether or not the surgeon is correct in his evaluation of Captain Vere's mental state.

The fatal event has occurred at the worst possible time. The fact that it is so "close on the heel" of the suppressed mutinies requires extraordinary leadership ability from a commanding officer, and as well, the skills of prudence and vigor, which Melville notes are "qualities not readily interfusable."

Billy's mortal blow has caused guilt and innocence to become "juggled," for now Billy has become the guilty agent of destruction, and Claggart the victim of violence. This is the case according to law, despite the fact that the victim had sought to victimize the criminal.

Captain Vere, who is known to be a man of "rapid decision," decides that caution is more important than speed in dealing with the matter presently before him. He decides to keep the incident confidential until its outcome is finalized. Some of his colleagues will later criticize Vere for his secrecy.

Captain Vere would much prefer to confine Billy and turn him over to the admiral once the *Indomitable* rejoins the fleet. However, he is acutely conscious of his duty as commander. Furthermore, he realizes that his crew will very shortly become aware that something is amiss, and that any delay in disposing of the problem would possibly incite them.

Thus he decides to convene a drumhead court composed of the first lieutenant, the captain of the marines, and the sailing master. He is concerned about choosing the captain of the marines, who is not, strictly speaking, a seaman. Although he is a reliable soldier in battle, Vere is not sure that bravery translates into ability for solving a moral dilemma.

He has no such concerns about the first lieutenant and the sailing master, who understand seamanship and the "fighting demands of their profession."

Billy is arraigned, and Captain Vere is the sole witness against him. "Concisely," Vere tells the entire story, omitting nothing. Billy is asked, and answers, that the captain's version is absolutely true. However, Billy adds that he is not guilty of Claggart's charges. Vere says that he believes him. Billy is overcome with emotion and stammers, "God will bless you for that, Your Honor!"

Billy testifies that he had no malice toward Claggart and did not mean to kill him. He explains that he was unable to verbally respond to Claggart's false charges, and that "I had to say something, and I could only say it with a blow, God help me!"

Billy is asked why Claggart should have lied against him, and Billy cannot answer. Vere comes to his aid, pointing out that only Claggart can know what was going on in his own mind. He adds that Claggart's motive is immaterial, and that the only issue that matters for the court is the outcome of Billy's blow.

Vere says that heretofore he has been functioning merely as a witness in the case. Since he notes the court's hesitation to decide the matter against Billy, he feels compelled to act as coadjutor. He commends the officers for their compassion, which he shares. However, duty demands that he "strive against scruples."

He urges the officers to acknowledge their doubts and to deal with them. He asks, rhetorically, "How can we adjudge to...shameful death a fellow-creature innocent before God?" Their aversion

to do so is "Nature," but their allegiance is not to Nature but to the King. The King's officers have given up the option of behaving as "natural free agents" and are obliged to obey maritime law.

The captain of the marines points out that Billy intended to commit "neither mutiny nor homicide." Vere agrees, but reminds him that such a plea has no import in a martial court which operates under the law of the Mutiny Act. Under that law, Billy's intent is of no consequence.

Vere asserts that they must either convict or acquit, but they cannot convict and mitigate the penalty. He fears that mitigating the penalty would seem arbitrary or weak-kneed and might lead to further mutinies.

Although the officers do not fully agree with Vere, they are loyal "lieges." Besides, they are influenced by Vere's concern for how their decision will be perceived by others.

Billy is convicted and sentenced "to be hung at the yardarm in the early morning watch."

Analysis

With the opening words of Chapter 22, "Who in the rainbow can draw the line where the violet tint ends and the orange tint begins?", Melville uses the rainbow as a simile for the fine line between sanity and insanity. Vere's sanity has been doubted by the surgeon, and later, by the officers of the drumhead court. They wonder about the mental state of a man who can go against his natural conscience to condemn someone who is innocent in the eyes of God.

Simile is used again where Vere's "vow of allegiance to martial duty" is compared to a monk's "vows of monastic obedience." Vere's rigid military discipline has been alluded to in previous chapters.

Melville emphasizes once again the significance of the historical context of "the unhappy event." It occurs "close on the heel" of the mutinies, a period "very critical...from every English sea commander...prudence and rigor." Although he is aware of Claggart's role in precipitating the crime by his own falsity, Vere is not legally allowed to "determine the matter on that primitive basis."

The captain of the marines notes that there is no one who might "shed light...upon what remains mysterious in this matter."

Vere replies that it is a "mystery of iniquity," which only a theologian can comprehend. This statement reprises Melville's digression in Chapter 12.

Despite the perception on all sides of Billy's innocence, he is condemned to death as a sacrificial lamb to ensure the peace and tranquility of the British fleet.

Study Questions

1. What is significant about the time period when Billy's fatal action occurs?

2. Why does Captain Vere decide to hold a drumhead court rather than wait and refer the case to the admiral?

3. Why does Vere have doubts about the suitability of the captain of the marines for serving on the drumhead court?

4. What explanation does Billy give for striking the fatal blow?

5. How does Vere behave while the court is deliberating?

6. Why does Vere intercede and declare himself a "coadjutor"?

7. Why are the officers told to act against Nature?

8. Why does Vere refuse to allow a verdict of guilty with a mitigated sentence?

9. Why are the officers persuaded to do as Vere wishes?

10. What is the outcome of the trial?

Answers

1. Since it "came on the heels" of the Great Mutinies, the law is very harsh, and the courts inclined to deal severely with infractions.

2. Captain Vere is concerned that a delay will create tension and dissent among the crew and might possibly arouse mutinous activities.

3. The captain of the marines is a soldier rather than a sailor, and he may not understand the traditions and ethos at sea.

4. Billy says that he couldn't speak so the only way he could respond to Claggart's false charges was to strike a blow.

5. Vere is visibly apprehensive, pacing to and fro.

6. He believes the officers are reluctant to act decisively.

7. Having taken an oath for their commissions, they owe allegiance to the King, not to Nature.

8. Maritime law does not take into account the motive of the perpetrator of a crime.

9. There are two reasons: loyalty to Vere, and also their concerns about how the verdict will appear to others.

10. Billy is found guilty and sentenced to hang from the yardarm.

Suggested Essay Topics

1. In your opinion, did Captain Vere do the right thing by persuading the court to find Billy guilty? From the issues mentioned in the text, defend or critique Vere's actions.

2. How does the historical context of the case impact on the outcome? What do you think the court's decision would be if the events were to occur nowadays?

Chapters 23–24

Summary

Captain Vere personally informs Billy of the court's decision. The interview is private, but knowing the character of each man involved, we can guess what took place.

It is likely that Vere would be totally frank, even admitting the part he himself played in bringing about the verdict. Billy would appreciate with "joy...the brave opinion of him implied in his captain making such a confidant of him." At the end of the interview, Captain Vere would very likely have allowed himself to feel those fatherly emotions toward Billy which his stoical nature usually concealed.

After the interview, when Vere exits the cabin in which Billy is confined, the senior lieutenant observes that Vere's suffering appears to be greater than that of the condemned man.

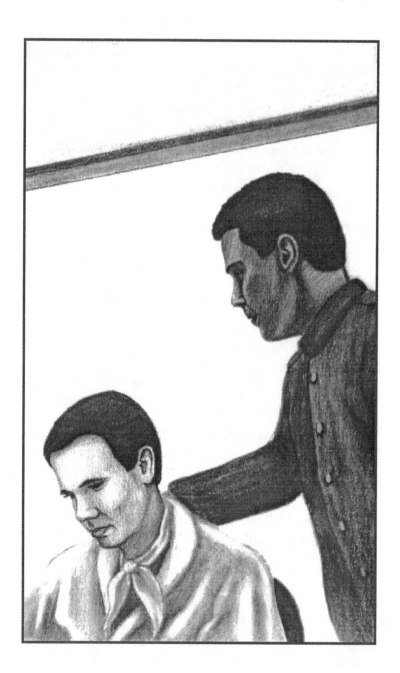

Less than an hour has elapsed since Claggart's accusation against Billy. In that short span of time, Billy has been tried, convicted, and apprised of his fate by Captain Vere. It is time enough, however, to arouse suspicions among the crew. A warship is like a small village, with rumor spreading rapidly. The seamen are not at all surprised when they are called to the deck for an announcement.

The sea is calm, and a full moon lights the deck wherever it is "not blotted by...shadows...thrown by fixtures and moving men." The marine guard, "under arms," lines up on either side of the quarter deck. Vere stands surrounded by his wardroom officers, his manner characteristic of his "supreme position." Concisely, he tells all—"the master-at-arms dead;...(Billy Budd) tried...and condemned to death;...the execution would take place in the early morning watch." Captain Vere never mentions the word "mutiny."

At the end of Vere's speech, there is a "confused murmur," which is quickly "suppressed by shrill whistles of the boatswain and his mates..."

Afterward, the body of the master-at-arms is committed to the sea with proper military honors. Propriety is strictly observed, for to deviate from custom would beget "undesirable speculations."

For the same reason, all communication between Vere and Billy Budd have ended, and the condemned man is beginning the "ordinary routine preliminary to the end." There are no unusual precautions taken, since there is the wish to impart to the crew that no trouble is expected. The sentry guarding Billy has orders not to allow anyone but the chaplain to speak with the condemned man.

Analysis

Melville cites the biblical story of Abraham and Isaac to describe Vere's emotions when he is about to condemn and sacrifice Billy Budd. Vere knows that Billy is innocent, but the best interests of the fleet demand that he deal harshly with any and all infractions. Billy is to be the lamb, but he will have no staying hand of God to intervene.

Melville's descriptions, and his attention to color, light, darkness and contrast, are especially significant in these chapters. The scene where Captain Vere addresses the crew evokes an eerie image of stark, dark shades (the clear-cut shadows of "fixtures and moving men") erupting into the light. It is a scene full of ominous portent.

The hierarchy of authority on board a maritime ship can be discerned by the men Vere surrounds himself with during his announcement to the crew. He is virtually encircled by "all the wardroom officers," while on either side of the quarter deck the marine guard stands with drawn arms.

Study Questions

1. Why can we assume that Captain Vere tells the complete truth to Billy Budd during their private interview?

2. What can we imagine of Billy's reaction?

3. What can be surmised about Vere's feelings for Billy?

4. Why does Captain Vere refrain from mentioning the word "mutiny" when he addresses the crew?

5. Why is Captain Vere concerned at this time for strict adherence to custom?

6. Why does Vere discontinue all communication with Billy?

7. Why does Vere prefer that the men not even surmise that something is amiss?

8. How do the officers behave on a military ship when they are concerned that something might be "amiss"?

9. How is Billy safeguarded while waiting for the sentence to be carried out?

10. Who is permitted access to the cabin where Billy is held?

Answers

1. That Captain Vere is an honorable and honest man has already been established by Melville's descriptions.

2. Billy would be joyful at being considered brave enough to hear all of the truth.

3. Vere apparently has fatherly feelings for Billy.

4. Vere doesn't want to arouse the crew by suggesting that he has concerns about mutiny.

5. By behaving as is customary, the crew will not find anything amiss.

6. It is the appropriate thing to do at this time.

7. If the crew surmises that something is amiss, that fact alone might actually foment trouble.

8. The officers "keep that apprehension to themselves."

9. Billy is held in a cabin guarded by a sentry.

10. Only the chaplain is permitted to have access to Billy.

Suggested Essay Topics

1. Explain how Vere's condemnation of Billy is comparable to Abraham's sacrifice of Isaac.

2. In Chapter 22 we are told that sailors are an obedient lot. How does this fact impact upon Vere's decision to stick to customary protocol in dealing with the aftermath of the crime and the trial?

Chapter 25

New Character:

The Chaplain: *he ministers to Billy, who is awaiting execution*

Summary

On the *Indomitable*, the uppermost deck is, for the most part, uncovered and exposed to the weather. Consequently, it is not a place where sailors go to spend their recreational time.

The starboard side of the upper gun deck is where Billy is lying, in chains, in one of the bays between the heavy guns.

The guns, carriages, and most everything else on the upper gun deck are painted black. Melville describes Billy's appearance. His "exterior apparel, white jumper and white duck trousers,...

more or less soiled...(glimmers) like a patch of discolored snow in early April..." Two battle lanterns flicker with dirty yellow light, polluting the "pale moonshine."

Billy lies there, just as much the Handsome Sailor as he has always been. His agony, his "young heart's virgin experience of the diabolical..." has passed, having healed in his private interview with Captain Vere. He looks like a "slumbering child."

The chaplain comes upon Billy lying in dreamy innocence. He realizes that his services are not needed—there is nothing he can offer that can transcend the peace which he beholds on Billy's reclining figure.

In the early morning, the chaplain returns. Billy, who is awake now, welcomes him. The chaplain is worried that Billy does not truly understand what death is. Although when he is questioned, Billy acknowledges that he knows he is soon to be executed, he appears to have only a childlike grasp of death.

Billy does indeed understand death, but he has no fear of it. The chaplain attempts to convey the ideas of salvation and a Savior, but the discussion is too abstract for Billy to follow.

The chaplain, being a man of good sense as well as good heart, does not persist. He withdraws, but not before kissing the condemned man on his cheek.

The chaplain is convinced of Billy's innocence, yet he does nothing to protest the terrible sentence. He believes that for him to do so would be futile. Furthermore, any such intervention is "beyond the bounds of his function."

Analysis

Melville describes the soiled snow-white figure of the condemned man lying against the black of the upper gun deck, like "a patch of discolored snow in April lingering at some upland cave's black mouth." Billy's figure is not pure white, but rather, slightly soiled white: the lamb's innocence is somewhat tarnished by his violent and destructive act.

Billy doesn't fear death because he is unsophisticated, a "barbarian." The barbarian is closer to "unadulterated Nature" than is the worldly, civilized man. Melville equates Goodness with the innocence of Nature, and Evil with the corruption of society. The Good

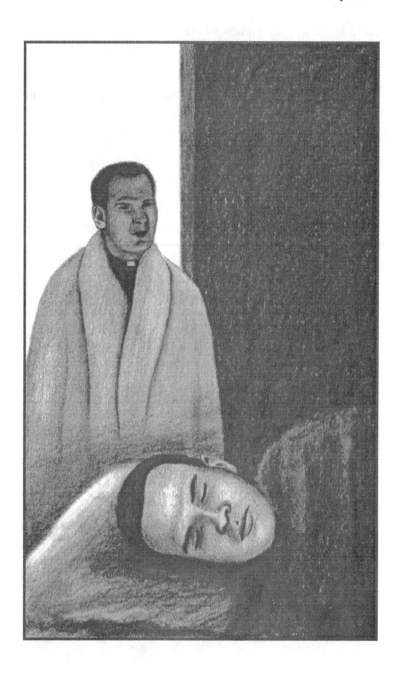

barbarian has no need of the artificiality of religion— his innocence is "even a better thing than religion wherewith to go to Judgment."

The problematic figure of the chaplain is implicit in Melville's depiction of an inherently good man, "a minister of the Prince of Peace," who is nevertheless "serving in the host of the God of War— Mars." The chaplain's function in the British navy is to subvert "the religion of the meek" to the uses of "brute Force."

Study Questions

1. Which deck on a warship is most exposed to the elements?

2. Where is Billy held pursuant to the execution?

3. What is Billy's demeanor as he awaits his execution?

4. What are the chaplain's thoughts about Billy as he observes him sleeping?

5. Why does the chaplain return in the early morning?

6. What does Billy think about death?

7. In what way is Billy like a barbarian?

8. What is Billy's response to the chaplain?

9. Why does the chaplain kiss Billy on the cheek?

10. Why does the chaplain not lift a finger to help Billy?

Answers

1. The upper gun deck is the one most exposed to the elements and the weather.

2. Billy is held on the upper gun deck to await execution.

3. Billy is as serene and peaceful as an innocent child.

4. The chaplain realizes that he has nothing to offer Billy that can soothe him, since Billy has already attained inner peace.

5. The chaplain wishes to impart to Billy an understanding of death.

6. Although he understands that he is about to die, Billy has absolutely no fear.

7.   Like a barbarian, Billy is closer to unadulterated Nature. Billy also looks like the Angles, barbarian converts to Christianity.

8.   Billy is attentive and polite, although he does not fully comprehend what the chaplain is saying.

9.   The chaplain comprehends that despite his crime, Billy is a morally good man.

10. The chaplain is conflicted—he is both in the spiritual service of God and in the employ of the British navy.

Suggested Essay Topics

1.   The chaplain is an ambiguous figure. Write an essay reflecting upon the conflicting roles he must play as a minister of God and as an officer of the British navy in wartime. Can those two roles be reconciled? Explain your answer.

2.   In what way is Billy a "Noble Savage"? What is Melville's understanding of the morality of the uncivilized man? Cite the text in formulating your answer.

Chapters 26–27

New Character:

The Purser: *he discusses the "singularity" of Billy's death with the surgeon*

Summary

At four in the morning, whistles blow to summon all hands to the deck to witness Billy's punishment. They come pouring onto the deck, quickly filling up all the spaces. Even the boats and booms are filled with crewmen, the topmen line the "sea balcony," and the marines fill the quarter deck. Captain Vere faces forward from the break of the poop deck.

At that time in the navy, executions were usually held from the fore yard. However, Billy's execution takes place on the main deck.

Billy is brought up to the main deck, with the chaplain attending him. The chaplain's manner toward Billy conveys the "genuine Gospel," rather than any sermonizing words.

Final preparations are made. The rope around his neck, Billy astounds everyone by blessing Captain Vere. He speaks clearly without stammering, saying "God bless Captain Vere." These words have a "phenomenal effect." Billy's "rare personal beauty" appears "spiritualized now..." In unison, and without apparent volition, the crewmen respond, "God bless Captain Vere."

As these words are said, Captain Vere stands rigidly erect, demonstrating stoical self-control.

The signal to complete the execution is given just as the ship is recovering from a periodic roll to leeward. At the same time, a vapory cloud hangs low in the eastern sky, "shot through" by the sun's rays, "like the fleece of the Lamb of God seen in mystical vision." In that setting, Billy is yanked up by the halter.

It has been scientifically established that a muscular spasm is "more or less invariable" at the point of complete bodily suspension. However, to the wonder of all, Billy's ascending body, with "the full rose of dawn," hangs motionless.

At the moment of execution there is utter silence. All that can be heard is the sound of the sea awash against the ship. The silence is gradually displaced by a strange, remote murmur. A command is given to "Pipe down the starboard watch..." The boatswain and his mates blow their whistles, piercing "that ominous low sound." The sailors soon disband.

In a digression, Melville recounts the attempt by the purser and the surgeon to understand the strange phenomenon of the motionlessness of Billy's hanging body. They are unable to account for this extraordinary occurrence.

Analysis

Melville uses a biblical reference as a simile: the coming of dawn is "like the prophet in the chariot disappearing in heaven and dropping his mantle to Elisha, the withdrawing night transferred its pale robe to the breaking day." The image symbolizes the transference of spiritual power from the heavens to the mundane world. The figure of the prophet Elisha is analogous to that of Billy Budd, the incarnation of simple holiness on earth.

Billy's last words, "God bless Captain Vere," are described metaphorically as "syllables...delivered in the clear melody of a singing bird on the point of launching from the twig." Billy too is on the point of "launching," literally, from the deck with a rope around his neck, and figuratively, from this life to a more spiritual existence.

Billy's spirituality is emphasized throughout his ordeal. The chaplain perceives his natural saintliness as the "true Gospel." Billy's forgiveness of Captain Vere is Christlike, similar to Jesus asking the Father to forgive his executioners.

Spirituality is again implied in the crew's echoing "God bless Captain Vere," which suggests the response of a church congregation.

In the discussion between the purser and the surgeon, Melville hints that the strange phenomenon of the lack of muscular spasm to Billy's body might indicate a kind of euthanasia, that is, Billy has somehow achieved a merciful death.

Study Questions

1. What are Billy's last words?

2. What is the effect of these last words upon the crew?

3. What action is taken by the ship's authorities when the murmur arises among the crew?

4. What is unusual about Billy's execution?

5. What is the effect of the circling sea fowl upon the sailors?

6. Why do the sailors respond the way they do to authority?

7. What question does the purser later discuss with the surgeon?

8. How does the surgeon know Billy's body ought to have exhibited a muscular spasm?

9. How does the surgeon account for the absence of such a motion in Billy's case?

10. What does the surgeon mean by describing Billy's death as "phenomenal"?

Answers

1. Billy's last words are "God bless Captain Vere."

2. The crew responds with a "sympathetic echo," "God bless Captain Vere."

3. The ship's authorities issue the command to the boatswain to blow his whistle, drowning out the murmur of the crew.

4. Billy's dead body doesn't show the usual muscle spasms, but rather hangs motionless.

5. Being superstitious, the sailors are profoundly affected by the sea fowl.

6. The sailors are trained to be obedient.

7. The purser discusses the reason for the lack of a muscular spasm.

8. The surgeon personally directed that Billy's execution was to be scientifically conducted, and in such a case, there should have been a muscular spasm.

9. The surgeon is unable to account for the lack of a muscular spasm.

10. "Phenomenal" in this case means "extraordinary."

Suggested Essay Topics

1. Although Billy fully understands Captain Vere's role and responsibility in the verdict, he blesses him in his last mortal words. Analyze the import of these last words. What do they mean? How is Billy's blessing comparable to or different from the last words attributed to Jesus on the Cross —"Forgive them father for they know not what they do"?

2. In Billy's execution, does Evil triumph over Good? Explain your answer.

Chapters 28–29

Summary

The crew is convened once more, this time to witness the burial at sea. When this is completed, a "second strange human murmur" is heard, this time, however, blending with the sounds of the sea fowl circling the burial site.

The presence of the sea fowl has great significance for the superstitious sailors. (See analysis.) Deeply moved by this omen, the sailors begin to display an "uncertain movement," an infringement of naval decorum. The officers move quickly—they give the order and the crew is swiftly dispersed by a drumbeat. The sailors, long accustomed to military discipline, now stand "erect and silent."

On the return trip to England, the *Indomitable* engages in a battle with a French ship, the *Atheiste*. In this encounter, Captain Vere is wounded by a musket ball. He is put ashore at Gibraltar with the rest of the wounded. When Vere dies there, his last words are "Billy Budd, Billy Budd."

Analysis

An old sea legend imbues sea fowl with spiritual powers, that of transporting the souls of seamen straight to heaven. Therefore, the superstitious sailors are deeply affected by the coincidence of the circling fowl at the very moment of Billy's burial at sea.

The authorities, troubled by the disruption among the crew and concerned about a possible insurrection, deal swiftly with the "uncertain movement" and the "encroachment" evident after the burial. Melville has previously prepared the reader for the instinctive obedience of the sailors when the authorities do take action.

Just as he used irony in naming the merchant ship, the *Rights-of-Man*, Melville uses irony in naming the *Atheiste*, the ship that vanquishes Captain Vere.

Billy Budd is very close to Captain Vere's heart, even as he lies dying. As the attendant makes clear in his verbal report to the senior officers of the *Indomitable*, these words were "not the accents of remorse." Rather, they were the loving utterances of a dying man preparing for spiritual reconciliation.

Study Questions

1. What sound is heard from the crew at the moment of Billy's burial?

2. What is the reaction of the authorities to the low murmur?

3. How does the crew respond to the authorities?

4. What serves as Billy's coffin?

5. How does the crew behave at Billy's burial?

6. What is the significance of the sea fowl on the crew?

7. What is the outcome of the battle between the *Atheiste* and the *Indomitable*?

8. What happens to Captain Vere in that battle?

9. Where does Captain Vere die?

10. What are Captain Vere's last words?

Answers

1. A low murmur is heard from the crew at the moment of Billy's burial.

2. The boatswain and his mates blow whistles to "pipe down" the men.

3. The crew disperses.

4. Billy's hammock, weighted down with shot, serves as his canvas coffin.

5. The crew again begins a low murmur.

6. The seamen are superstitious, and they take the sea fowl as some sort of omen.

7. The *Indomitable* is victorious.

8. Captain Vere is seriously wounded.

9. He dies at Gibraltar.

10. His last words are, "Billy Budd, Billy Budd."

Suggested Essay Topics

1. How do Melville's descriptions of the scenes at Billy's execution and his burial affect your appreciation of the story? Cite relevant passages from the text.

2. The name of the ship with which the *Indomitable* is engaged when Captain Vere is mortally wounded is the *Atheiste*. What is the effect of this irony? Is Melville trying to say that spirituality is finally overcome by lack of faith? Take a position and cite passages in the text to back up your position.

Chapters 30–31

Summary

An account of Billy's execution appears a few weeks later in an official naval publication, but the report is full of misinformation and distortion, due, in part, to the factors of rumor and distance.

Under the heading, "News from the Mediterranean," the report reads, in part, as follows:

"...a deplorable occurrence took place on board H.M.S. *Indomitable*...the ship's master-at-arms, discovering...some sort of plot...and that the ringleader was one William Budd...in the act of arraigning the man before the Captain was vindictively stabbed to the heart by...Budd.

The deed...suggest(s) that...the assassin was no Englishman...

...the victim (was) a middle-aged man, respectable and discreet...

The criminal paid the penalty of his crime... Nothing amiss is now apprehended aboard the H.M.S. *Indomitable*."

This official version of the incident gravely distorts the characters of Claggart and Billy Budd. There is a quite different story making the rounds among the common sailors. For them, the events of Billy's life and death have become legendary. As with many legends, the tale becomes embellished, and Billy comes to

be regarded as a sort of holy saint. In fact, chips off the spar from which Billy was hanged are regarded as holy relics, in much the same way as chips of wood from Jesus' Cross are so regarded.

Although most of the ordinary seamen who were not immediately present or involved in the tragic events related here remain ignorant of the full facts of the case, they believe in Billy's essential goodness. They remember "the fresh young image of the Handsome Sailor," an image now imbued with mystery and sanctity. In death, Billy is glorified.

No doubt the strange and mysterious circumstance of his ascending body at his death greatly influence the embellishment of the stories that are making the rounds.

There is an acquaintance of Billy's, another foretopman from Billy's own watch, who happens to have some talent for writing poetic verses. In order to honor and celebrate the life of his heroic friend, he composes some appropriate lines to immortalize Billy's tragedy. The poem makes the rounds, and it is eventually printed as a ballad. It is given the title "Billy in the Darbies."

In this ballad, the poet attempts to tell the story from the point of view of the spiritually courageous hero and to imagine his thoughts as he is about to be executed.

Analysis

The legend of Billy's innocence endures, due in part to the valorization of Billy after his death.

Melville again demonstrates the human capacity to uphold opposing feelings or principles, despite the rational incongruities. On the one hand, the seamen who preserve the legend of Billy Budd agree with the judgment of Captain Vere, who despite his spiritual insight must obey the rules of worldly standards (the Articles of War). On the other hand, they fully understand the essential innocence of the tragic hero. They perceive that the three major players in this drama (Billy, Vere, and Claggart) will be judged by a higher standard. They also perceive that by a heavenly standard of judgment Billy is without blame. Thus Billy lives on, eternalized in the memory of the common sailor. It is noteworthy to what extent those hardened veteran seamen allow themselves to be emotionally touched by Billy Budd.

Study Questions

1. Where did the written account of the execution appear?

2. What reason does that account give for suggesting that Billy was not an Englishman?

3. How is Billy described in that account?

4. How is Claggart described?

5. What object becomes a relic for the seamen?

6. What image of Billy Budd remains in the hearts and minds of the sailors?

7. Who is the author of the ballad written about Billy's death?

8. From whose point of view is the story told in the ballad?

9. What is the title of the ballad?

10. How do the official account and the sailors' memories differ?

Answers

1. An account of Billy's execution appears in an authorized naval publication.

2. In that account it is suggested that Billy was not an Englishman because of the vileness of the murder and the reported murder weapon, a knife.

3. Billy is described as a criminal of extreme depravity.

4. Claggart is described as a respectable and discreet man, who was brave and patriotic.

5. The spar from which Billy was hanged, as well as any chip from that spar, become relics.

6. They remember "the fresh young image of the Handsome Sailor."

7. One of the other foretopmen from Billy's watch writes the lines for the ballad.

8. The story the ballad tells uses Billy's point of view.

9. The ballad is titled, "Billy in the Darbies."

10. The official account finds Billy guilty, whereas the sailors remember Billy as the innocent party.

Suggested Essay Topics

1. Explain the process by which Billy's life and death have become legendary. Cite events from previous chapters that possibly contribute to the legend.

2. Pretend you are a reporter for the official naval publication that carried the news of Billy's execution. Write a brief but accurate account of that event.

Sample Analytical Paper Topics

Topic #1

Discuss the conflict between Good and Evil in *Billy Budd*. Consider the historical and geographic contexts for the various events in which the conflict between Good and Evil is expressed.

Outline

I. Thesis Statement: *The setting for* Billy Budd, *aboard a ship in wartime, provides a world in miniature where the complexities of the conflict between Good and Evil unfold dramatically.*

II. Impressment

    A. Justification for impressment in wartime

    B. Injury to personal freedom

    C. The "Good" vs. the "Evil" aspects of impressment

III. The shipboard culture

    A. Ordinary seamen vs. the officers

    B. Obedience

    C. Billy's difficulties aboard the *Indomitable*

    D. Dansker's explanation

IV. The mutinous plot

    A. Foreshadowing and context

B.   The offer to Billy

C.   Billy's response

D.   Claggart's evil intent

V.   False accusation

A.   Foreshadowing, where Claggart is compared to the Rev. Titus Oates

B.   Historical/political climate

C.   Claggart's charges

D.   Billy's anger and response

E.   The reversal of Evil and Goodness

VI.   The verdict

A.   Guilt or innocence

B.   Wartime exigency

C.   Spiritual Good vs. Worldly Duty

VII.   Attitudes toward death

A.   The natural man

B.   The sophisticated man

Topic #2

Discuss the character of each of the three protagonists in this story—Billy Budd, John Claggart, and Captain Vere. Explain the personification of Good and Evil as they appear respectively in Billy and Claggart. Explain the conflict between spirituality and devotion to martial duty within the heart of Captain Vere.

Outline

I.   Thesis Statement: *The three protagonists, Billy Budd, Claggart, and Vere, respectively personify Innocence, Evil, and the worldly mediation of moral duty.*

II.   Billy Budd

A.   The Handsome Sailor

      B.   Mysterious origins

      C.   Innocence

III.   John Claggart

      A.   Mysterious origins

      B.   Rapid rise

      C.   Aversion to Billy

      D.   Essential depravity

IV.   Captain Vere

      A.   Comparison with Lord Nelson

      B.   Convictions

      C.   Superior intellect

      D.   Conscience vs. Worldly duty

V.   Who is the real hero of *Billy Budd?*

      A.   The near-perfection of Billy Budd

      B.   Captain Vere's human torment and its resolution

Topic #3

Discuss the biblical references throughout *Billy Budd.* Explain the source contexts for at least three of those references and the meanings for the similes and metaphors that Melville employs.

Outline

I.   Thesis Statement: *The biblical references serve to cast Billy Budd as a hero of spiritually epic dimension. Billy is portrayed as a Christlike figure, an innocent sacrifice for the sins of humanity, who remains blameless throughout his ordeal.*

II.   Adam before the fall

      A.   Natural faith

      B.   Innocence

III.   Mysteries of Iniquity

      A.   God's inscrutability

    B.   Second coming of Christ
IV. Saul and David
    A.   Love and jealousy
    B.   Attraction and repulsion
V.   Ananias
    A.   Conspiracy
    B.   Divine judgment
VI. Abraham and Isaac
    A.   The favored son
    B.   Sacrifice of the innocent
VII. Billy as the Christ figure
    A.   For the good of all
    B.   Ascension

Bibliography

Quotations from the novella *Billy Budd* have been taken from the following edition:

Melville, Herman. *Billy Budd and Other Tales* (based on the text edited by F. Barron Freeman and corrected by Elizabeth Treeman c. 1948, 1956) Signet Classic edition. New York: American Library, 1979.

Other Sources:

Allen, Gay Wilson. *Melville and His World.* New York: Viking Press, 1971.

Anderson, Charles. *Melville in the South Seas.* New York: Columbia University Press, 1939.

Bercaw, Mary Kay. *Melville's Sources.* Evanston: Northwestern University Press, 1987.

"Billy Budd." In *The Oxford Companion to English Literature.* 5th ed. Edited by Margaret Drabble. Oxford: Oxford University Press, 1985.

Bloom, Harold, ed. *Herman Melville.* New York: Chelsea House, 1986.

Dillingham, William B. *Melville's Later Novels.* Athens and London: University of Georgia Press, 1986.

Franklin, H. Bruce. *The Wake of the Gods: Melville's Mythology.* Stanford: Stanford University Press, 1963.

Hillway, Tyrus. *Herman Melville*. New York: Twayne Publishers, 1963.

"Melville, Herman." In *Benet's Reader's Encyclopedia*. 3rd ed. New York: Harper & Row, 1987.

Miller, James E., Jr. *A Reader's Guide to Herman Melville*. New York: Farrar, Straus, and Cudahy, 1962.

Pullin, Faith, ed. *New Perspectives on Melville*. Edinburgh: Edinburgh University Press, 1978.

THE BEST TEST PREPARATION FOR THE

AP

ADVANCED
PLACEMENT
EXAMINATION

ENGLISH
Literature & Composition

by Pauline Beard, Ph.D. • Robert Liftig, Ed.D. • James Mohr, Ph.D. •
James Maloney, M.A. • Joanne Miller, M.A. • Peter Trenouth, M.A. • Mattie Williams, M.A.

6 Full-Length Exams

➤ Every question based on the current exams
➤ The ONLY test preparation book with detailed explanations to every question
➤ Far more comprehensive than any other test preparation book

Includes a COMPREHENSIVE AP COURSE REVIEW,
emphasizing all areas of literature & composition found on the exam

REA *Research & Education Association*

Available at your local bookstore or order directly from us by sending in coupon below.

REA's Test Preps
The Best in Test Preparation

REA "Test Preps" are far **more** comprehensive than any other test preparation series
Each book contains up to **eight** full-length practice exams based on the most recent exams
Every type of question likely to be given on the exams is included
Answers are accompanied by **full** and **detailed** explanations

REA has published over 60 Test Preparation volumes in several series. They include:

Advanced Placement Exams (APs)
Biology
Calculus AB & Calculus BC
Chemistry
Computer Science
English Language & Composition
English Literature & Composition
European History
Government & Politics
Physics
Psychology
Spanish Language
United States History

College Level Examination Program (CLEP)
American History I
Analysis & Interpretation of Literature
College Algebra
Freshman College Composition
General Examinations
Human Growth and Development
Introductory Sociology
Principles of Marketing

SAT II: Subject Tests
American History
Biology
Chemistry
French
German
Literature

SAT II: Subject Tests (continued)
Mathematics Level IC, IIC
Physics
Spanish
Writing

Graduate Record Exams (GREs)
Biology
Chemistry
Computer Science
Economics
Engineering
General
History
Literature in English
Mathematics
Physics
Political Science
Psychology
Sociology

ACT - American College Testing Assessment

ASVAB - Armed Service Vocational Aptitude Battery

CBEST - California Basic Educational Skills Test

CDL - Commercial Driver's License Exam

CLAST - College Level Academic Skills Test

ELM - Entry Level Mathematics

ExCET - Exam for Certification of Educators in Texas

FE (EIT) - Fundamentals of Engineering Exam

FE Review - Fundamentals of Engineering Review

GED - High School Equivalency Diploma Exam (US & Canadian editions)

GMAT - Graduate Management Admission Test

LSAT - Law School Admission Test

MAT - Miller Analogies Test

MCAT - Medical College Admission Test

MSAT - Multiple Subjects Assessment for Teachers

NTE - National Teachers Exam

PPST - Pre-Professional Skills Tests

PSAT - Preliminary Scholastic Assessment Test

SAT I - Reasoning Test

SAT I - Quick Study & Review

TASP - Texas Academic Skills Program

TOEFL - Test of English as a Foreign Language

RESEARCH & EDUCATION ASSOCIATION
61 Ethel Road W. • Piscataway, New Jersey 08854
Phone: (908) 819-8880

Please send me more information about your Test Prep Books

Name _____

Address _____

City _____ State _____ Zip _____

MAXnotes®

REA's Literature Study Guides

MAXnotes® are student-friendly. They offer a fresh look at masterpieces of literature, presented in a lively and interesting fashion. **MAXnotes®** offer the essentials of what you should know about the work, including outlines, explanations and discussions of the plot, character lists, analyses, and historical context. **MAXnotes®** are designed to help you think independently about literary works by raising various issues and thought-provoking ideas and questions. Written by literary experts who currently teach the subject, **MAXnotes®** enhance your understanding and enjoyment of the work.

Available **MAXnotes®** include the following:

Absalom, Absalom!
The Aeneid of Virgil
Animal Farm
Antony and Cleopatra
As I Lay Dying
As You Like It
The Autobiography of
    Malcolm X
The Awakening
Beloved
Beowulf
Billy Budd
The Bluest Eye, A Novel
Brave New World
The Canterbury Tales
The Catcher in the Rye
The Color Purple
The Crucible
Death in Venice
Death of a Salesman
The Divine Comedy I: Inferno
Dubliners
Emma
Euripedes' Electra & Medea
Frankenstein
Gone with the Wind
The Grapes of Wrath
Great Expectations
The Great Gatsby
Gulliver's Travels
Hamlet
Hard Times

Heart of Darkness
Henry IV, Part I
Henry V
The House on Mango Street
Huckleberry Finn
I Know Why the Caged
    Bird Sings
The Iliad
Invisible Man
Jane Eyre
Jazz
The Joy Luck Club
Jude the Obscure
Julius Caesar
King Lear
Les Misérables
Lord of the Flies
Macbeth
The Merchant of Venice
The Metamorphoses of Ovid
The Metamorphosis
Middlemarch
A Midsummer Night's Dream
Moby-Dick
Moll Flanders
Mrs. Dalloway
Much Ado About Nothing
My Antonia
Native Son
1984
The Odyssey
Oedipus Trilogy

Of Mice and Men
On the Road
Othello
Paradise Lost
A Passage to India
Plato's Republic
Portrait of a Lady
A Portrait of the Artist
    as a Young Man
Pride and Prejudice
A Raisin in the Sun
Richard II
Romeo and Juliet
The Scarlet Letter
Sir Gawain and the
    Green Knight
Slaughterhouse-Five
Song of Solomon
The Sound and the Fury
The Stranger
The Sun Also Rises
A Tale of Two Cities
Taming of the Shrew
The Tempest
Tess of the D'Urbervilles
Their Eyes Were Watching God
To Kill a Mockingbird
To the Lighthouse
Twelfth Night
Uncle Tom's Cabin
Waiting for Godot
Wuthering Heights

RESEARCH & EDUCATION ASSOCIATION
61 Ethel Road W. • Piscataway, New Jersey 08854
Phone: (908) 819-8880

Please send me more information about MAXnotes®.

Name _____

Address _____

City _____ State _____ Zip _____